T0194128

Here, Jesus

. . . Catch!

JEAN SMITH

WESTBOW
PRESS®
A DIVISION OF THOMAS NELSON
& ZONDERVAN

WestBow Press books may be ordered through booksellers or by contacting:

WestBow Press
A Division of Thomas Nelson & Zondervan
1663 Liberty Drive
Bloomington, IN 47403
www.westbowpress.com
1 (866) 928-1240

ISBN: 978-1-9736-2876-7 (sc)
ISBN: 978-1-9736-2875-0 (e)

Print information available on the last page.

WestBow Press rev. date: 09/13/2018

To my husband, for loving me and all the sacrifices you made.
To Mr. Ezra, chaplain at a hospital in Northeast Texas for following
The Lords lead to inspire this book
To my mom and dad, whom I love and miss with all my heart,
And finally, to my sister Arlene who passed away as the book was
Finished and she was so proud of me.

PREFACE

Why? Is there anyone else who has experienced any incident in their life where you didn't ask why? Why me, Lord? Why is the Lord doing this to me? This question plagues many of us. As you read, you will see you are not alone in this journey through life.

I would like to thank some very special people who have supported and encouraged this endeavor. They believed my story would help others. The little bird's cage has been opened and she is ready to fly, by the grace of God! There are so many people in life who have struggled with and suffered through many of the same things I have. Perhaps, like me, the struggles keep coming. I pray you will be encouraged by my story. I want to show people that God is with us all the time. I pray I might intrigue you and give you hope in Jesus Christ our Savior.

I believe I have been inspired by the Lord to share how Jesus caught my child's heart and held me throughout the years. Some of it may seem unbelievable and harsh, but it's meant to show each person who reads this book that they can overcome adversities no matter what happens in any stage of life. I have experienced many things, but I did not express a lot due to sparing my family any hurt.

I have had weaknesses and strengths in many areas of my life. I put no glory in my words; all of the glory goes to my Father in heaven. When I enter my final destination, I can imagine him opening his hands to welcome me home with a little pink flower petal in his hand. This book is not meant to sugarcoat the problems we go through in life. It is not saying that being a Christian makes you exempt.

Hurt and pain hit every walk of life, but I am living testament that you can overcome. It may be a slow process, but it will come. Patience has never been my best virtue, but you can't rush God on anything. It will all be in his time and his purpose. When that happens, you will know because you will have perfect peace.

CHAPTER 1

Life as We Knew It

"For I know the plans I have for you," declares the LORD, "plans to prosper you and not to harm you, plans to give you hope and a future."
—Jeremiah 29:11 (NIV)

Jeremiah was known as the weeping prophet. He was a major prophet in the Bible, but I suppose you could say he was a complainer. Maybe you could relate better to a crybaby. Man, I can relate to him. Jeremiah resisted the call by complaining that he was only a child and did not know how to speak.

Jeremiah 1:6

> However, the Lord insisted that Jeremiah go and speak, and he touched Jeremiah's mouth to place the word of the Lord there. God told Jeremiah to "Get yourself ready."

I was told many years ago that I should write a book, and I laughingly said I didn't believe my story was unique enough to tell. Her reply was that it would have to be written as fiction because nobody would believe a lot of the life I've lived. I thought she was kidding and just assumed everyone had similar memories. My story goes way back. If you trust the Lord and wait on him, he will catch you too.

Have you ever thought you were destined for greatness? Are you one of those fortunate people who experience worldly greatness, success, money, happiness, and contentment? Have you thought you were destined for a life of hurt and pain due to circumstances beyond your control? Nobody thinks their life is really going to be so chaotic. There are lots of things we can control that we choose not to.

Everyone goes through hurt and pain in life, but some experience it way more than others do. My life seemed to be destined for hurt and pain. Not every instance in my life has been hurt and pain, but the things I have had happen to me have been devastating at times.

In life, you can choose to be a victim of your circumstances or be an overcomer. I chose early on not be a victim, but for years, I fell into that pattern. In my twenties and thirties, I chose to be an overcomer instead of a victim.

The Lord knows I fell into that victim mentality many times. Anyone can make that choice if they truly want it, but only God can heal the wounds and turn a victim into an overcomer. Unfortunately, this is something you must work at all of the time. Once you have been a victim, it's easy to fall prey to that again. It can be a daily choice, but there is a victorious woman or man inside you. You have to choose! Even when we choose another way in life, God knows the path we are to take. That is why he urges us to make ourselves ready!

I did not have a perfect childhood, but we were loved and taught to be respectful. My parents loved us as they were taught to love. Like many families in the sixties, I grew up with the idea that going to work with my momma was normal. She was a bartender and a waitress. I had a bed under the bar and a huge playground on the dance floor. That was normal life for my family.

I participated in the entertainment. They would give me any beer that was left in the bottle, and I would dance around with a lit cigarette in my hand. My mom said I could sit there and make up the best stories. She said I made them laugh and had an amazing imagination, but I am not sure where it went!

As I entertained while getting the family drinks on the house, I thought that was the life. Today, that would be totally unacceptable, but times were different back then. My dad had various jobs but was a painter by trade. He was a kind and gentle man, but he loved his liquor as well.

Unfortunately, my parents were alcoholics, and for the most part, that came first. If you have a family like that, you know what I am saying. My mom and some of her family members occasionally talked about church, but they were mostly pretenders. I didn't know what that was, but it did not leave much room for conversation about Christianity, the church, or Jesus. It was not mentioned much unless a cousin was making fun of Christianity. If the occasion presented itself to go to church—if the bus came around—I could go. Otherwise, we were not exposed to it.

My parents didn't raise wimps. We are tough, and we are fighters for life. In our family, it was expected to do what the elders said—regardless if it was what you agreed with or wanted. When I was young, we moved so much. It was no big deal for me, but I am sure it was a big deal for my siblings. We moved nearly twenty times in five years. I turned into a little wallflower with little stability.

When I was three, we lived deep in south Texas. My oldest sister, Arlene, was nineteen when she had her first child. JC and I were two and a half years apart and constant companions. One day, my sister and I were playing outside by a huge pink oleander bush. Out of the clear blue, I ran and grabbed a handful of those flowers. I ran back to play and started spinning around and around. I finally threw the petals up in the air and screamed, "Here, Jesus ... catch! Little did I know how that would set a precedent for my life. I still didn't have a clue about God or Jesus. From that point on, a love for Jesus was planted in my heart. I had no clue why, but my love for Jesus began growing daily. Ever since then, I have loved him so much.

Here Jesus…Catch

CHAPTER 2

On the Go

Not long after leaving a small border town in Texas, we moved to a small town not far from other places my parents had lived before I was born. There was a beautiful man-made lake all the way around where we lived. That was the nicest home I remember living in. However, we had to ride the bus forty miles to school. It was often stop and go, and I got motion sickness every day. I failed the first grade there because of my motion sickness. However, I have many good memories of living there as well.

Once, my sister and I decided we were going to go scouting. We came to this cliff and decided to climb around on it. This cliff was high; had we fallen, we would not have been found for a long time. We walked along the edges like professional rock climbers. The Lord no doubt gave his angels charge over us.

A few months after I had settled into that little town, the time came for another move. We moved to a small coastal town in Texas. The main thing I remember was going to vacation Bible school for the first time, and Daddy came to the final program. I was so excited he was there. I wanted to tell him what I had learned about a man named Jesus.

I came down with measles, and my sister had the German measles. We were not there for long. When I was six, we moved about thirty miles away to a much smaller coastal town. In that town, many things about my life would change in a short time. We lived in three different places in that small town. I made friends who I am still in contact with. Ann named her daughter after me, using my complete first and middle name.

I thought she would find a better middle name, but I cherish the fact that she loved me that much.

Theo and Rodney and the Bautista boys created some of my most wonderful memories. We played outside all day until dark. We lived next to a railroad track with large gravel pits next to it. We had some fun sliding down those gravel piles. We always had to borrow cardboard from the boys down the road. We loved that because they would want to come and out play with us.

Jesse and Eddie were closest to our age, and Theo was about three years older. We were all best friends, and most of the time, we were more like family. We would do kid things like hiding in crates and waiting to be found or stealing a peck on the cheek for the very first time. We were always welcome at the Bautista home.

Ms. Dee's door was always open to any of us. Don't tell anyone, but I think she liked me best. Looking back, I realize that she made each one of us feel that special. I remember her kindness and the smell of fresh tortillas and beans in her home. She was always so sweet to us, and being poor themselves, she always let the little stragglers in for food. We were all very poor, but when we went to her home, we would run through her kitchen and grab one or maybe two tortillas and then run off again. There was no need for cups back then. If you wanted a drink, everyone's local water hose was up for grabs. I don't remember going to school much, but I remember playing a lot at that age.

Oh Jesus....please Catch

CHAPTER 3

Time to Grow Up

For it is written, "He will command his angels
concerning you to guard you."
—Luke 4:10 (NIV)

When I was older, I was the designated babysitter. My sisters were old enough to get jobs, and Mom bartended during the day. Daddy worked nights.

When I was about seven years old, I babysat for the first time alone for four or five kids. Looking back now, I see that I was a mere baby, but that was what we deemed normal. On one of the nights I was babysitting, we had all gone to bed. My nephew was nine months old, and I fell asleep beside him. Suddenly, to my surprise, I was yanked out of the bed and onto the floor.

Everyone was in a panic.

I had rolled over on my nephew, and my aunt and uncle had gotten home just in time! He had already turned blue and was close to death. I got in a lot of trouble for that before I understood what had happened.

After I got my first spanking, I never wanted to be a disobedient child again. I was a good kid. I was still very shy, but the Lord continued to watch after these little misfit kids, molding us and strengthening us for the things that would befall us later on.

I have worked very hard in my adult life to avoid and break that vicious cycle. I was still the young entertainer in my family, and as a young woman, I was attending bars and parties with my family. But as I grew older, my personality changed. I stopped being an entertainer or a partier. I had no more of that childlike thinking. I was about to learn the realities of life.

I was so shy that it was hard to imagine I had done all that entertaining. I thank the Lord daily for my two sisters. Starlet is ten years older, and Lola is four years my senior. When I was young, they were my constant overseers. When they found jobs, I was left with the privilege of going with Momma and Daddy. There was generally a host of others to go with to a party at the beach or at little dive bars. In our small town, my parents were frequent patrons, so we knew many people from that style of life.

We never stayed in one place for long, and there are many memories that I have forgotten—or that I suppressed because of trauma. The Lord was rescuing me again, and I didn't even know it. I prefer to focus on the great memories of being with my parents. My mom taught me to dance on her feet, and I learned how to swim in the Frio River on my momma's back. Daddy grew cantaloupe just for the two of us in his immaculate and lush gardens.

One day, a couple missionaries came to the house. I was playing outside, and they wanted to know whether I would talk to them. Since we had seen them before, it wasn't like I was talking to strangers. I was very shy and didn't know what to say. Instead, I listened carefully to them. They told me about Jesus and about how much he loved me. That day was my salvation experience, but I did not truly comprehend all the details. After they left, I sat against the back of the house, put my face in my hands, and cried. I knew I had asked Jesus to enter my heart. I had a wonderful feeling inside. You can only get feeling through a salvation experience. I will not forget that day even though I did not comprehend what it all truly meant.

As I was going into fifth grade, we had to move to east Texas, which was where my parents were from. I still vividly remember everything about our stay on Maglan Street. Our small house was gray, and it had another building behind it. I don't remember whether some of the sisters lived back there or if it was storage. I climbed on top of that building many times, dangling my legs and working up the nerve to jump down. It seemed so far down, but it was less than six feet.

Unbelievably, that house is still there more than fifty years later. It the same color, and the same building is behind the house. Mr. and Mrs. Bautista still live in the same home, and she still has the same cooking pot on her stove from all those years ago.

Here Jesus...Catch

CHAPTER 4

Why Lord?

Be heard not seen. Be strong and courageous. Do not be
afraid or terrified because of them, for the LORD your God
goes with you; he will never leave you nor forsake you.
—Deuteronomy 31:66 (NIV)

One summer, we went to visit my sick aunt in a small border town in Texas
where we used to live. She was dying from cancer, and my mom would go
there every chance she had to help take care of her.

During one of our visits, my niece and I wanted a snow cone from
the stand down the street. We got our little money together, and when we
placed our order, we didn't have enough money. Since the worker at the
stand had already made them, one of us had to run back home and get
the rest of the money. I stayed, and my niece ran to my aunt's house to
get more money.

It was a hot day, and I was barefoot. I assumed the man's invitation
to come in the cool air was a nice gesture. The man told me I could come
in the cool air and wait for her to get back. I went inside, which was a big
mistake. He immediately pulled me down on his lap and began to put his
hands under my clothing. I tried to get up, but he was too strong.

My niece showed up with the rest of the money just before anything
more could happen. As I walked out the door, the man told me that he
knew where I was staying, and that if I told anyone what he'd done, he
would come get me. Thinking I may have done something wrong, I never

told anyone. If I had told my mom, as I look back on it now, she would have gone down there and likely beat him. But I was a child, and children believe things like that.

Today, I know something done to a child is not their fault. And threatening to hurt one's family is something they say because they don't want to get into trouble themselves.

"All who fear the LORD will hate evil. Therefore, I hate pride and arrogance, corruption, and perverse speech" (Proverbs 8:13 NIV).

Let those who love the Lord hate evil. Those of us who love the Lord and love our children hate evil, and we do all we can to protect our kids from it. I realize there are much worse things than this, but it was confusing, hurtful, and scary to a little girl. I wish I had said something. I have regretted not saying anything for so long. That man scared me for life. From that point on, I believed every older man was like that. I cringed every time an older man besides my daddy hugged me. It stayed with me, but I have found forgiveness for that man. I can only pray that he came to know Christ at some point.

My sweet aunt finally succumbed to cancer after she had fought and suffered so much. We had some really good times with her; she was a flaming redhead. When she was not ill, she was a true fireball. She had an identical twin, and they were two of the funniest women I ever met. They also loved their drink, and if there was any difference between them and the rest of our family, it was that they were extremely loyal to each other and their family.

When I was a young teenager, just beginning to look like a young lady, a family member held me down and touched me in all the inappropriate places. I never told anyone because of who it was. Nobody would have believed it. I kept quiet once again.

I began to wonder what I was doing to cause those things to happen. I became even more withdrawn around friends and family. Many times, people turn toward the things that happen to them instead of running from them. They want to be pleasers, and they think that is what they are supposed to be like for approval. I, on the other hand, always avoided certain people who made me feel uncomfortable.

He who dwells in the shelter of the Most His will abide in the shadow of the will rest in the shadow of the Almighty. I will say of the LORD, "He is my refuge and my fortress, my God, in whom I trust." Surely he will save you from the fowler's snare and from the deadly pestilence.
—Psalm 91:1 (NIV)

Here Jesus…Catch

CHAPTER 5

Little Eyes Are Watching

I was raised in a very musical family. My dad and his siblings were talented musicians, and my dad played in his own band when he was younger. Several family members have gone to Nashville, and it wasn't because of a lack of talent that they didn't make it.

When it came to singing, my niece was the shining star out of all of the grandkids. My mom showed her off whenever she could. She started to sing she was very young when. My oldest sister also had an amazing voice.

When I was asked to sing, I would act like I couldn't because I was scared of rejection. I began to grow in the shadows. I was a cute little wallflower. I was shy and withdrawn, and I never reached for my own dreams. In my young to late teens, I did not realize God was in control at all times.

I grew up around alcoholism, verbal abuse, and physical abuse. As the youngest of six kids, I saw and experienced way less than my siblings did. Sadly, domestic abuse happens to men as well as women. And my dad was an abused spouse. He would try to avoid altercations, but therein lays the perils of alcohol. He would shield himself, and he wouldn't hit back. I would see him so messed up that he would tell people he was robbed or was in an accident. I wanted so badly to take care of him, but when they fought, we were not allowed to talk to him. If we did, we would get in trouble.

> Woe unto them that rise up early in the morning, that they follow strong drink; that continue until night, til wine inflames them. (Isaiah 5:11 NIV)

The fights always stemmed from drinking and partying. I used to think of him not fighting back as a weakness, but after I began to mature, I realized it took more for him to stay than it would have to leave. Codependency is often learned, and I was always watching, which is where I first saw that pattern.

> And one who has experienced His loving forgiveness cannot help but love and forgive others. Christian husbands are commanded to love their wives as Christ loved the Church. (Ephesians 5:25 NIV)

My parents knew how to push each other's buttons. I really pray that she realized the love he had for her after fifty-three years of marriage. My mom could be very loving and kind, and she would help anyone. However, after drinking, she could become hurtful and cruel with her words. There were times I wished she had gone ahead and gotten it over with instead of cutting me with her words. She also loved with all her might, and she would have defended us to the death.

My three older siblings were long gone, but my other two sisters were always close by to make sure I was okay and had what I needed. As a teenager, I started going to small beer joints with Momma and Daddy. By the end of the night, someone was fighting. Someone in our family always came home with war wounds.

I loved—and continue to love—my mom and dad. If I could have them back right now, I would. However, I wish I had had better memories from growing up. There were times when good things happened. We always had great Christmases. We didn't have much, but they managed to make it seem like we had a million dollars.

People tend to block out traumatic things because that is what the mind does for protection. It was not a normal upbringing, but substance abuse and domestic violence are more common today than most people realize. That is why a relationship with Christ can be your salvation. Almost everyone thinks life is normal or perfect. Praise the Lord.

CHAPTER 6

Settling In

I guess I could say that I am from East Texas since that was where we stayed the longest. I began fifth grade there. There was a lot of old money there. Since we were poor, we were not socially accepted. However, I made lasting relationships and grew far beyond what I could have ever imagined.

A special family literally changed the course of my life. My friend Jo and I met when a group of us were swinging across a creek bed by their house in the nice neighborhood right around the block from where we lived. Leave it to me to not let go of the rope in time and get hurt. Jo took me to her house like a wounded bird, and Mrs. Gipson fixed me right up.

A bond began that is still a vital part of my life. Everyone needs a family like the Gipsons in their lives. Their home became my home away from home. It was a refuge for me. We became so close that they would buy my school clothes and pay for me to vacation with them. They were so good to me.

"A man of many companions may come to ruin, but there is a friend who sticks closer than a brother" (Proverbs 18:24 NIV). Jo was like a sister and a best friend to me. Our relationship grew, and they may as well have adopted me. When we would compare our suntans after a day in the sun, I was always darker because Jo was so fair.

They had dogs named Pity Pat and Dandy, and when we lay out, they tanned with us. Herman was a pet frog who lived in ivy on the hearth. They would feed him and water him, and he never left his spot. I'm not sure how old Herman was when he passed, but his memory and bones remain in Jo's safe.

We would leave my house, hide my clothes behind the air conditioner, and ask if I could stay the night. The answer was always yes. A skating rink came to town and was the main hangout for a long time. The skating rink was not far from where we lived. It was a tent rink with wood floors. We had some fun times there. Jo and Andrew were the daredevils on skates, but nobody could beat us on the hokey-pokey!

Any time I was at Jo's house, my dog was with me every step of the way. Whiskers came with us from the coast. The most important thing the Gipsons did for me was introducing me to church, faith, and Christianity. I always had the love of God, but I finally found the Jesus I threw those petals to.

If you don't work on your faith and Christianity, you never learn or grow. I was a teenager, and I didn't realize how much the Word of God means. They may never know the impact they had on a young girl's life. I loved that family. Jo was two years older than me, and we grew apart after she graduated and started nursing school. I missed them so much, but life had to move forward. I saw them frequently, and my love never died.

The Gipsons taught me most of the things I've learned about life. They even mentioned girl things. The topic of sex—or anything like it—was not spoken of in my house. If you needed to know what to expect on a date, Mr. Gipson would answer any question we had—no matter how hard it was for him to answer.

Mrs. Gipson was such a quiet, gentle woman. I loved her fried chicken, and Jo loved my mom's fried chicken. Her carpet was always raked amazingly. They had the most unique refrigerator with flower contact paper all over it. It was amazing, and I wanted to use contact paper on everything! Mrs. Gipson was always taking care of everyone else. I cannot imagine what my life would have been like without them in it, but I know the Lord had me in his hands.

> Therefore encourage one another and build one
> another up, just as you are doing.
> —1 Thessalonians 5:11

CHAPTER 7

Let the Games Begin

We had more weekend get-togethers than you could imagine for the whole family, our friends, and their kids. We always had great time, but there was always lots of alcohol. As children we had so much fun because it was a normal life for us. My mom and her baby brother would always have the get-togethers. My cousins and I were close, and we were close in age as well.

My cousin David was Mr. Athlete, and his dad was very proud of him because he was good at everything. I was very good at running. I think my speed came from running away from the rooster that was always chasing me. When they would come down, the race was on. Once the wagers were made, we had to race. David was also the fastest in his school, so my uncle was sure he would beat me every time. Just like the rooster, David could never catch me.

He begged me to let him beat me once so my uncle would stop making us do those silly races, but I told him no way because I would have to listen to my momma. We kept racing, and I still never let him win. We still laugh about it, and he says he never realized how a girl could be so fast.

At one point, I was an Olympic hopeful. Since we were poor and did not know what resources to look for, my parents never gave it another thought. I didn't make a big deal of it, and they had no clue how much I wanted that dream. Once again, my dreams were crushed. I never believed that my dreams were achievable. It didn't come as a huge surprise since I knew they could not afford anything like that. I mourned my lost dream in silence.

When I was in junior high, the school formed a flag football team for the girls. My friend and I were two of the better players. Rooster was aggressive, and I was fast. Her brother Russ was one of our coaches, and he was one of the best-looking guys in the school. He was sweet as could be, But he and "Rooster" went at it all the time, hence I nick named her Rooster, because she and her brother would go at it like two roosters fighting. I still call her that to this day, what a wonderful friend.

One day while practicing in their backyard and as her brother was telling us what to do, he taught me how to catch and dodge. The play was made and here he comes to grab my flag, well I was so shy and yet wanting him to tackle me at the same time, I just couldn't do it, so I went down out of embarrassment to be tackled. I say this because as much as I was becoming a young lady, it was still engrained in me that it was not normal to feel those things that made me feel embarrassed and dirty if I did anything the opposite of what I was taught.

And I am sure of this, that he who began a good work in you
will bring it to completion at the day of Jesus Christ.
—Philippians 1:6 (NIV)

CHAPTER 8

My Other Mothers

When I had two years left in high school, my mom and dad decided to move to south Texas for daddy to be a foreman on a large ranch. I did not want to leave. I was in many activities and moved in with my sister. Starlet would never admit it, but what a hardship that had to have been on her to be a single parent with no help and take on another teenager to care for. She never wavered, and we developed a bond that has only grown stronger over the years. I have the utmost love and respect for her. She has done so much for me and always wanted the best life had to offer me.

> Love is patient and kind; love does not envy or boast; it is
> not arrogant or rude. It does not insist on its own way; it is
> not irritable or resentful; it does not rejoice at wrong doing
> but rejoices with the truth. Love bears all things, believes
> all things, hopes all things, and endures all things. (1
> Corinthians 13:4–7 NIV)

I also stayed a lot with Lola and her family. She never wavered on taking me in and helping when and where she could. I admire and love her for all she did for me as well. "Love bears all things, believes all things, hopes all things, endures all things" (1 Corinthians 13:7).

I was very naive and believed whatever people told me. My family had many laughs at my expense. They were not trying to be cruel or mean. Since I was so gullible, they would take advantage of me. We had a conversation about who would walk to the store to get some sodas. I'm not sure where the conversation got twisted, but I ended up at the store to purchase strawberries, grapes and oranges. When I returned to the house with grapes and oranges, explaining that they didn't have strawberries because they were not in season, everyone began to laugh.

I was confused when they asked what had happened to the sodas they were waiting on.

I felt so silly, and to this day, it is still a topic of conversation. Everyone started laughing, and I said, "Well, I got what ya'll asked for."

I chose to sink my time into my school activities, and I dedicated my time to my passion, which was running. Most of the time, I would run to the Gipson's home because it was like my sanctuary. Contentment always brought fun and love and peace.

CHAPTER 9

Love Is in the Air

I was at the lake one weekend with my sister and her friends when a blond-haired, blue-eyed dreamboat pulled up in a gold Impala. Oh, my. Yes, love at first sight does happen. From that moment on, we were inseparable. The only catch was that I was fifteen. I could not date until I turned sixteen—and then I had to have a chaperone. David and I dated from ninth grade until senior year. We had so many good times as teenagers. We had lots of double dates, fusses, and breakups.

We had a double date one night with my longtime friend, Kynlee. However if you wanted to do anything—even eating out—you really needed to go to Kilgore. The next town over was wet, and Henderson was a dry county. A Friday night date was going to eat pizza and getting a beer for David. He loved pizza and beer, and if we were lucky, we got to go to the drive-in, which my parents never knew because I would have been in so much trouble.

On one double date, I was angry at my family because they were all going out. I was no longer old enough to go to the bars—I was in the in-between age—and when David and Ray got there, I told him we wanted to go out and get drunk. He tried to talk me out of it, but I said I wanted to know what the big deal was.

We went to Kilgore, and I had a few drinks of wine. I became violently sick and swore I would never do that again—if I lived. "Be not quick in your spirit to become angry, for anger lodges in the bosom of fools" (Ecclesiastes 7:9).

That one night made me despise alcohol, and I never made it a part of my lifestyle.

We were closing in on graduation, and I had enough credits to graduate midterm. In the summer before my senior year, David asked my parents if he could marry me. We wanted to get married in August. As the baby—and the only family member to graduate—my parents were not ready for me to get married.

David had to promise my mom that he would make me graduate. He was tougher on me than my parents ever were. I went to school until Christmas break and went back and walked with my graduating class. We married in August 1978; sixteen months later, we had a baby girl. Before I got pregnant, the doctor told me I might not be able to have children. He said we might want to go ahead and try because it could take a while. God's timing was perfect. I was pregnant the next month. We were so ecstatic to be parents and a happy newly married couple.

I can do all things through him who strengthens me.
—Philippians 4:13 (NIV)

CHAPTER 10

Squeeze Three Times

Two months after she was born, we took her to her first checkup. My brother was in town, and waited for David to meet us at Mom and Dad's house. When he got there, my brother wanted David to ride his horse for exercise. David didn't want to ride. He just wanted to see his baby girl, but my brother could be relentless.

While David saddled up and began to ride, my sister and I decided to take a jog in the pasture where he was riding. Suddenly, the horse came up behind us so fast—and I realized David could not control the horse. The horse went through the only patch of woods in the pasture.

David was not an experienced rider. The tree limbs began to hit him in the face. When instinct kicked in, he jerked to the side, hit a tree with his head, flipped off the horse, and landed on the ground. I thought he was dead because it knocked him out. When we rushed over to him, he tried to get up. My brother had driven the truck down to the pasture, and David got up and walked to the truck. He went into the house, washed out his mouth, and realized he had almost bitten off his tongue.

He thought he was okay, but we went to the hospital anyway. As we got closer to the hospital, he began to get worse. His head was aching, and he was nauseous. When we got to the hospital, they began testing that showed he had a fractured skull that would require immediate surgery. He was placed in an ambulance and taken to Tyler for two major surgeries.

When we dated, we were told we could not do more than hold hands. Our sign to say I love you was to squeeze each other's hands three times. As they put him in the ambulance, he was beginning to go into a coma. I was trying to keep him from pulling the tubes out of his nose, and I grabbed his hands to hold them. I was crying and trying to talk to him, and he squeezed my hand three times before he fell into a deep coma.

Those were the longest days of my life. I felt so lost, yet he was just down the hall. On Friday night, friends from work, from youth, from school, and family were lining the halls in support.

Kynlee was there, but I was still a fog. I had not left the hospital in case he woke up. That day, he had improved slightly.

David's mom was going to go home for more clothes and a little rest. She told me goodbye and said she would see me early in the morning. After a few minutes, I saw her in the main waiting room. At first, I thought she had forgotten something, but she never came back.

I asked Kynlee if she would go find out why David's mom had come back.

When Kynlee came back, she had a different look on her face.

I asked if everything was okay.

She shrugged, but I could tell something was wrong. I asked her to tell me the truth.

She began to cry and told me they called David's mom back because he had taken a turn for the worse.

I ran back to the double doors, but they stopped me. It was too late. He had passed away. After two major surgeries on his brain, he died three days later. I went into shock, and I don't remember anything until my mom woke me up to go make arrangements. I fell apart. I was a single parent and had lost my love.

> For if we live, we live to the Lord, and if we die, we die to
> the Lord. So, then, whether we live or whether we die, we
> are the Lord's. (Romans 14:8 NIV)

One of the most memorable and wonderful gestures my mom did for me occurred on the morning we were to go to make arrangements for the funeral. I looked at her and asked her for a favor. She said, "Anything."

I asked that there be no alcohol on the hill during this time. Could she do that for me? When there was a death in the family, it was customary to celebrate their life after the funeral with lots of alcohol to kill the hurt and pain. I wanted no part of that. It was not a time of celebration to me, and I wanted it treated as such.

My mom kept a watchful eye to make sure my wishes were honored, and they were. I don't think my family ever drank so much coffee. The only way I got through time was because the Lord covered me with his grace. When you experience the death of a loved one—a kind, gentle, loving soul who loved life—you cannot help but question God. I did many times. Sometimes I would get an answer, but most of the time, it was just questions followed by anger, severe sadness, and loneliness.

The Lord eased me slowly through the process of loss. I may never understand the process of death of such a young person with so much to live for, but God does—and each person goes through it differently.

Ecclesiastes 3:1–8 (NIV) says it best, particularly in verse 4: "A time to weep and a time to laugh, a time to mourn and a time to dance."

But the Lord knows our time and our ways are not His. And that is a hard pill to swallow because when you want an answer, you want an answer.

Oh Jesus Please ....Catch

CHAPTER 11

Growing Up

He sets on high those who are lowly, and those
who mourn are lifted to safety
—Job 5:11 (NIV)

We may have only been married for a short time, but it was the love of a lifetime. What was I to do? I had a two-month-old baby! I don't know what I would have done without my family and Jo. I was totally in a fog, and it didn't lift for quite some time.

When David passed away, his family was equally devastated. The process of grief is different for everyone, and it was very different for much of his family. Jelaine was just an infant, and I had a very hard time letting her out of my sight.

David's family and I had always had a decent relationship. I would take Jelaine by to see her grandmother, but as it went on, it clearly became too emotional for her. She finally told me I needed to wait for a spell before I came back because it was just too hard to see her right then. She had been a very hands-on, wonderful grandmother, and I suppose that was what I had hoped she would be for Jelaine. However, that would not come to be.

David's family began to distance themselves from us. Many times, I would get angry and say, "She is all you have left of him—why do you not want to be in her life?" It hurt me so much. When I remarried, it basically ended our relationship. I never really understood the situation, but I had no choice in the matter. I don't believe there was a blame game or anything because it was just a freak accident. I think that was just how they coped with it.

I received some very sound advice from my sister's husband. He was also David's best friend. He said, "Let them talk to her when they call, and if she asks, let her call them. They will eventually come around or they won't. If they don't, at least Jelaine will always know that you always tried to place her in their lives, that you never discouraged her from having a part of them, and it was their choice."

Unfortunately, the correspondence became less frequent. We were still living in the same town. To this day, she still has no contact with his family.

When I married Cal, he had the most remarkable parents. They never treated Jelaine as a step-anything. She was just as important to them as any of their blood relatives. She had amazing substitute grandparents, and I will be grateful for them forever.

CHAPTER 12

Time to Run

About a month after David passed away, I was an emotional wreck. I called a man I looked up to for counsel. I had known him as a spiritual leader for years. He invited me to his home, so we could have some counsel and prayer time together. I left Jelaine with my mom and headed over to their home.

When I got there, his wife was gone. Since he was a "spiritual mentor," nothing out of the ordinary ever crossed my mind.

He welcomed me in, and we sat in his den. I poured out all my questions. I was crying while I poured my heart out to him. He got up from his chair and came across the room to sit beside me.

I trusted him completely, but all of a sudden, he began to tell me how his needs at home were not being fulfilled. He told me how attractive I was, and he began to touch my leg and rub my back! I began to die inside. This man I loved and admired was making a pass at me. All I could think at that moment was about how I was going to get out of there. Praise God. In a nick of time, we heard a car drive up.

He jumped up and went back to the other side of the room.

When his wife came in, I jumped up and told them I needed to get home to my baby.

Since I had been crying so much, his wife insisted that he show me how to get home. He led me to my mom and dad's house, but he stopped right before their driveway and walked over to my car.

I was so nervous, and I barely rolled down my window.

He wanted to kiss me good night.

Ugh. No! Once again, I kept that quiet for a while. When he came by to check on me, I ran and hid like a child. I begged my mom to tell him I was not home because I did not want to see him.

After he left, my dad looked at me and asked me in not-so-nice words what that man had done to me.

When I told them nothing, they both knew I was lying. I eventually told them, and they were the only ones who ever knew except Jo.

> Beware of false prophets, who come to you in sheep's clothing, but inwardly are ravening wolves looking for whom they may devour. (Matthew 7:15 NIV)

Don't get me wrong. I in no way want to categorize every spiritual leader in a bad light. There are many more great leaders out there than tainted ones, but we must remember that the enemy can grab hold of anyone, especially those who are trying to live for the Lord. They are human too and fight the flesh daily.

I have forgiven that man, but it had lasting effects on my heart and life.

My mom and Lola were right there to help me and teach me the rights from wrongs of being a new mommy, but they were just as bad as I was about spoiling her.

After a few months, I thought the two of us would take a trip. In reality, I was running away from the pain. I went back to some of my old roots. I went to see my sister in Port Lavaca. She helped me with babysitting and tried to encourage me to go to the beach or go do something. I suppose my moping was getting old.

As we were coming home from the beach one day, we decided to go down our old street and see the Bautista family. Wow! We talked, caught up, and renewed our friendship.

Jesse had become a Christian by then, and we began to talk daily. He started counseling with me, praying with me, and reaffirming that God was still there for me. He was not used to being around babies, and he called Jelaine La Ratita (little rat) because she was so small. We would go to the park, and he would automatically begin to read the Bible to me. I was right where God wanted me to be—and I didn't even know it.

I fell in love with Jesse, but I thought I was betraying David's family. It was too soon after David's passing. I wondered who put the time limit on loss and grieving. I was twenty years old with a baby, and all I knew was that it felt good to be with someone who loved me and that I loved. I allowed my family to dictate what was acceptable.

As summer came to an end, we drifted apart. Jessie and I would remain close, but my life had to get back to whatever my normal was about to become. I had not been home since March 3, 1980, and everything was exactly the same. I had to grow up and be an adult.

CHAPTER 13

An Emotional Roller Coaster

It would have been a great time for Jesus to catch me.

Jo knew I was in a bad way emotionally. My family would take care of Jelaine, and she didn't need me. Although I loved her more than life, I was so depressed I wanted to die. Jo worked with a man named Cal, and she kept trying to fix us up. He was going through a divorce and finishing seminary, and she knew I needed someone to talk to.

I finally relented and agreed to meet with him if she would come as well.

They came in with a six-pack of Dr. Pepper for our visit. I was mortified. I had technically only dated two men, and I had married one of them. *I loved and lost him—and now she wants me to meet someone?*

Cal wanted to take us to eat, but I was reluctant. It took some talking to convince me to leave the house. Jelaine was almost a year old, and she was very spoiled. She acted up during the outing. I had emphasized to Jo that there would be no kissing—I wouldn't have any of that.

When it came time for him to leave, I was scared he would try to kiss me. I thought I would die right then. As he got to the door, he turned, extended his hand, and shook my hand.

I turned to Jo and said a huge thank you for telling him not to kiss me. She informed me that she had not told him.

I was a bit taken aback. *Well, what is wrong with me that he wouldn't even try to kiss me good night?* I guess I didn't know what I was thinking either way. I was attracted to him because he didn't push me. There were times when he would call and want to talk or go somewhere, and I would be too depressed to go. He would not let that slide and would give me a hard time.

After a few more double dates, I decided it was time for a solo trip. We went to eat and became exclusive. We dated for three months before we were married.

It was a whirlwind romance. And to top it all off, my family hated him. They wanted nothing to do with him because they felt like I was betraying David. My emotions were running ninety to nothing. They actually called on our wedding day to beg me not to marry him. They were convinced it would ruin my life because it was too soon! I was young, and I had never gone against my family. I thought it was time to stand up to them once and for all. He had a boy and a girl, and we were about to blend our families. There was a lot of work to get settled in.

We had lots of good times and bad times. Our time started out like many others. We were in love and trying to make time for each other. I was contending with an ex-wife, and he was contending with a memory. I was barely a mom for the first time and was taking on two more kids. Needless to say, we were starting out with some real rough patches ahead.

We bought a small convenience store to support our family. A larger corporation came in and bought us out, which was a traumatic experience that turned out to be a good thing.

Once again, Jesus caught me.

The corporation came in and remodeled the whole store. We had a really sweet thing going, but we were not frugal with our profits. We were young and not financially savvy.

Cal had several jobs he outsourced from our store. I mostly ran the store, and Cal always enjoyed working with his hands, so he self- taught himself how to work on and install gas pumps, due to the type of work we were in. He has always been very resourceful in everything he has done. Much to our surprise, I became pregnant with the other light of my life. Nicole, my blue-eyed beauty, would melt our hearts.

About three months after finding out I was pregnant, my mom's brother passed away. He and my brother were the same age and were more like brothers than cousins. My brother was in a bad state of mind when my uncle passed. There was lots of alcohol. At the cemetery, my brother confronted Cal—who he hated with a passion—and told him to meet him behind the school so he could show him a few things.

The papers called it "The Shootout at the OK Corral."

My brother was waiting on him, and when he got there, my brother started to shoot.

Of course, Cal shot back.

> Let all bitterness and wrath and anger and clamor and slander be put away from you, along with all malice. (Ephesians 4:31 NIV)

About a year after that incident, my brother passed away at forty-six from a massive heart attack. He was the oldest and only boy, which would lead to my mother giving up on life. She grieved so hard for almost four years, and then she had a massive heart attack.

I was left with no momma. I felt so lost and so alone. I was the baby. It was a tough transition, but time does help. However, I have never stopped missing her.

As my parents aged, they mellowed a lot. The younger grandkids had great memories of Mammie and Papaw, and I am so thankful for that. However, they were still a part of the alcohol at the family get-togethers. As we all do when we get older, we tend to ease up on the things we seemed to deem important as disciplinarians. I often look back on those things as trivial.

Jesus said, "Let the little children come to me, and do not hinder them, for the kingdom of heaven belongs to such as these" (Matthew 19:13–14 NIV). When he had placed his hands on them, he went on from there.

CHAPTER 14

Pain Like No Other

Without counsel plans fail, but with many advisers, they succeed.
—Proverbs 15:22 (NIV)

We decided to sell the store and move to a small town called Laneville. If you blinked when you went through, you would miss it. We bought an old homestead house, remodeled it, and started a new business. We had a small convenience store there as well. Lots of changes began to take place, and we almost had everything right within our reach.

I was diagnosed with cervical cancer, which required a radical hysterectomy. The surgery was a success, and I did not have any treatments because they got all the cancer. With me being unable to work for a while, it gave us clarity to decide it was time for something more stable than owning our own business. It quickly became feast or famine, but it was famine way too frequently.

Cal's parents were two of the greatest people I've ever known. They moved in next door to us after we had been there a year. To this day, they remain two of my biggest heroes. Cal decided to go to nursing school, and I took on two jobs. When he got out of school, he would work in the emergency room for an extra paycheck. When he graduated, the entire family was so proud of his accomplishments.

He began working nights, and we were like two ships passing in the night. Three of our four children were living with us, and our fourth decided to leave her mom's home and join us. Blended families are tough.

Chris was such an amazing young man, and we had established a loving relationship. He loved his mother, but they had issues. She was always trying to tear our relationship apart. Blending in his sister should have been easy, but on Christmas in 1990, they went to spend the day with their mother—and she wanted to argue by trashing me. Chris got angry with her and stood up for me.

They left her house and came back to my parents' house while we were having our family Christmas. Chris was visibly shaken and told us what happened. They barely spoke again, which was a tragedy in itself.

> Let not your hearts be troubled. Believe in God; believe also in me. In my Father's house are many rooms. If it were not so, would I have told you that I go to prepare a place for you? And if I go and prepare a place for you, I will come again and will take you to myself, that where I am you may be also. And you know the way to where I am going. (John 14:1–4 NIV)

When I came home from work on February 25, Cal had already left for work. The three girls were attempting to cook supper.

Chris was sixteen and had his own vehicle parked in the driveway. I went into the house and talked with the girls for a few minutes before sitting down to rest. They wanted to serve me my supper. I asked them where their bubba was, and they said he had gone down to the feed store to see one of our friends.

As the time passed, I asked about Chris again. I called my mother-in-law to find out if he was there, but she had not seen him in a few hours. I became alarmed. We lived in a small town, and if he hadn't taken his truck, he couldn't be far.

I called some of his friends, but no one had seen or heard from him. We began a car search, and I made a call to Cal to tell him we could not find Chris. He said he would leave work and come home.

All our friends in the community searched for him.

I found out he was being bullied at school for defending his sister's honor—and another girl at school had tried to trick him into believing she might be pregnant. It was all a total shock to our systems, but our goal was to find Chris.

His grandparents decided to ride the ten acres of pasture that butted up against the church. They thought he might be playing basketball down there.

As they made their way back toward home, my mother-in-law noticed the door to the barn was open, which was odd. She got out of the truck to check it out, and our lives would change forever.

She saw his lifeless body in the dirt with a gun. He had committed suicide. No words can explain it other than God's grace came down and swept us up. He would have to hold us for a long time. Chris left no note and no explanation. There were no wet goodbye kisses—nothing. He was gone.

Cal drove up as the sheriff's department arrived. I tried to stop Cal from going in, but he ran to his son as fast as he could. He fell to the ground, grabbed him, cradled him like a baby, and screamed, "Not my son! Why my son? God, why?"

For eight months, I watched the man I love struggle with Chris's death. I was so focused on making sure our girls were ok, it would be about three years before I realized I had not yet grieved for Chris. I was too busy trying to take care of everyone else. I didn't realize then what a drastic turn of events would take place.

> Do not fear, for I am with you; do not be dismayed, for
> I am your God. I will strengthen you and help you; I
> will uphold you with my righteous right hand.
> —Isaiah 41:10 (NIV)

CHAPTER 15

Stages and Changes

But he said to me, "My grace is sufficient for you, for my power is
made perfect in weakness." Therefore I will boast all the more gladly
of my weaknesses, so that the power of Christ may rest upon me.
—2 Corinthians 12:9 (NIV)

That turn of events drew me closer to the Lord than I had ever been. I
stayed in a constant state of prayer as I watched Cal's gentle soul begin a
struggle like none I had ever seen. Suicide is the worst death anyone can
possibly deal with. There was no note and no explanation. With no valid
answers to your questions, the guilt goes straight to your head. Death is
inevitable, but when someone you love and care about chooses to end their
life, it totally changes the course of everyone involved.

Eight months passed with pleas to God, but Cal got no answers. He
went to the Word of God, but he found no peace. There are many stages
of grief, and if you get stuck in one or more of them, everyone else is stuck
with you. The first is denial. You cannot fathom that your child or the
person you love has made a choice to do such an unspeakable act. You look
for reasons. Maybe someone else did it to make it look that way. Maybe he
was goofing off, and the gun went off.

The second is anger. After eight months of stopping at the cemetery
every day on his way home, sitting until dark or later, Cal would come
home emotionally and physically drained. He commented once about

how—with his lawn chair and cooler of Dr. Pepper at the cemetery—he was only six feet away and could not touch his sixteen-year-old son.

As the anger began to well up inside him, we argued all the time. I think he would pick fights just to get away from us. He worked as an RN and began to hang out with the guys at the hospital, which was not a good thing. He transformed right before our very eyes. I sometimes would wait up all night, and he would not show up. He was riding a motorcycle, and all I could see was a death wish waiting to happen. He didn't care to live or die. It did not matter that his family needed him. He didn't see what he did to hurt us emotionally. He began abusing drugs and alcohol in an attempt to kill a pain that would never go away. I was oblivious for the most part. I was at another crossroads in my life. What was I to do?

> If any of you lack in wisdom, let him ask of God, who gives to all liberally and without reproach, and it will be given to him. (James 1:5 NIV)

Next comes bargaining. Whatever it takes, Lord, whatever you want me to do, I will give my life for his. Just give him back to me. Please, God. I need to see him once more and touch him once more. During this time, there is no resolve. The Lord knows the pain we are in, and he knows how long the process will last.

Next comes depression. It is so hard to get a man to admit that he is depressed. Cal cried all the time and went deeper and deeper into himself. And the deeper the depression, the more the other stages would appear. I often saw every stage of grief at the same time. Cal's depression and anger went hand in hand, and he did not know how to handle either one. He was in the deepest pit I had ever seen. After five long years, by the grace of God, the last stage began to appear.

The last stage is acceptance. With suicide, it's not always possible to reach the point of acceptance of the loss of your loved one. The entire family was trying to get through each of the stages, and all of us moved through each stage at our own pace. Cal went to counseling, but he saw no validation in it.

The counselor told Cal he knew how he felt, which was the wrong thing to say.

Cal was filled with anger and was ready to walkout—until the doctor told him his own son had committed suicide so many years back. At that point, Cal began to melt and cry.

That was not even close to where he needed to be, but it was a start.

You will have suffering in this world.
—John 16:33 (NIV)

CHAPTER 16

Trying to Regroup

It seemed like hardship was the pattern for my life. I was totally devastated and lost. I felt abandoned by God.

Cal's heart became hardened. His anger scared him, and he thought it would be better for him to leave for a while. We had a small travel trailer, and he moved to Longview, which was forty-five miles away. I was doing my best to hold down a full-time job and make sure the kids were okay. Cal came back and forth to see us before leaving again. He was running away from what we all had to face: Chris was never coming home.

Cal came home out of the clear blue one day and said we were selling our home. He had found a place in Longview, and we were moving. It was Christmas, and he had me go back to Laneville to get all the gifts and bring them to the new place. It was hard leaving Laneville, and we still had many trials to endure before it was said and done.

We were in Longview, but Cal was still in denial. His anger became worse. He bottled it up inside, and he blamed God. He questioned God and lashed out at him. The more we pushed for counseling, the more he ran from it. He was lost in total darkness, and that was right where the enemy wanted him to be. He walked away from all his morals and his moral obligations. He merely existed.

I waited and waited and waited. When the drug abuse became bad enough, I decided I needed to take the kids and leave. We moved out, and he stayed in our home. I had finally been released by God to leave the situation. We moved to an apartment and were doing the best we could.

He had called me one weekend to tell me he was going to a weekend getaway with "the guys." I was at the point where I didn't believe anything he said or did. I just wanted to be done. I wanted to heal from the hurt and move on. Once again, The Lord had other plans for us.

Though I could not see it, the Lord had already begun his handiwork.

> Behold, blessed is the one whom God reproves; therefore despise not the discipline of the Almighty. For he wounds, but he binds up, he shatters, but his hands heal. (Job 5:17–18 NIV)

Cal called me after about three months. I did not want to talk to him, but he insisted that we needed to talk. A mutual friend of ours had passed away, and Cal asked me to ride over to see the family. At first, I refused. When I relented, he said, "I'm going to get you back."

Inwardly, I laughed. Too much pain and hurt had passed between us, and I didn't believe we could heal. Over the next two weeks, he tried to win me back. The harder he tried, the harder I tried to ignore him.

He had a major relapse with the drugs, but he agreed to go back to rehab and really work the program. We moved back home to help him, which it was no easy decision, but after much prayer, I felt I was making the right decision.

I was outside my family's wishes again. They were furious that I would return to Cal. I had used my family as a sounding board, and it was hard for them to believe he was changing.

When I returned, there was a huge rift through the middle of my family. I was taught that blood came first. I was torn, but I straddled the fence and tried to please everyone.

I knew I had to follow God's Word and his commands and be obedient to him. I had prayed for our marriage to work for years. Since God had allowed that to happen, I had to try. It was not easy. It was probably one of the hardest things I've ever done. To this day, the memories and pain still haunt me, but I know God is in control.

> Trust in the Lord with all your heart and lean not on your understanding. In all your ways, acknowledge Him and He will carry you through.
> —Proverbs 3:5–6 (NIV)

CHAPTER 17

Only through God

Many people have asked, "Why are you staying? How can you stay?"

In no way was it within me to have the strength to stay. That strictly came from the Father. It took a toll on our marriage in many ways. I have always tried to glorify the Lord in everything I did. I have failed many times. I have doubted with the best of everyone, but he is loving and forgiving and understands our weaknesses. Thanks be to God. Psalms 27:14 NKJV "Yes, wait for the Lord; Be of good courage, and He will strengthen your heart, wait I say on The Lord.

I was thinking we were finally going to get our act together and be a family, but health issues are about to creep back in. I would end up questioning and praising the Lord again.

After I had my cervical cancer, I never missed an appointment or checkup, which was a good thing.

A few days after an appointment, my doctor called to inform me that my test had come back showing cancer cells. I needed to go back for more tests. I thought I didn't have to worry about that anymore since I had already had everything removed. That was a common misconception. I had a reoccurrence, and I had to do internal chemo for ten weeks.

That was a very scary time, especially with everything we had already gone through. Only the last five treatments made me sick, and I was given an all clear.

After all of the trials of Chris's death, we still had more to go through. About ten years after we moved from Laneville, we decided we wanted to exhume his body and move him to the family cemetery. After a year of red tape, we were given permission to move him. I was working on the day it was to take place, but Cal was there to observe the process.

Once they pulled the vault out of the ground and were ready to put it on the big truck, the lift stopped working. It stalled, and they had to wait for another truck to get there. It was getting late.

Cal had brought a flatbed trailer to transport the headstone, and he asked them to put the vault on his flatbed.

They didn't want him to do that, but Cal told them that he would be honored to transport him. It would be the closest he would be able to be to him until he was in heaven.

They loaded it up, and they left.

When I called Cal to find out how things were going, he told me what had happened. Chris was not mine by blood, but I loved him and believed he loved me. When it all happened, I was in a fog, which I like to think of as God's grace carrying me through the shock of the tragedy.

Cal was bringing Chris home, which was an honor bestowed him by the Lord. It gave him the closure he so desperately needed.

The reality is that people need to find their own peace. And it is within you because the Lord has put a story to share in each of our hearts. You may share in a small group, a large group, a woman's meeting, or a church. The possibilities are endless. If I can do this, anyone can.

The enemy was working overtime with me. I had to change a lot of my thoughts and ways of doing things. I was in another fog. I was trying to help Chris's friends, teachers, and family, yet I never took the time to grieve myself.

When Moses's hands grew tired, they took a stone and put it under him and he sat on it. Aaron and Hur held his hands up—one on one side, one on the other—so that his hands remained steady till sunset. Moses's arms soon became so tired he could no longer hold them up.
—Exodus 17:12 (NIV)

CHAPTER 18

Work It Out

Then your light shall break forth like the morning, your healing
shall spring forth speedily, and your righteousness shall go
before you; the glory of the Lord shall be your rear guard.
—Isaiah 58:8 (NIV)

It seemed like life was finally about to straighten up for us. Cal surrendered
back into the ministry, and we began our journey into very tough and
rewarding work. However, we found out very quickly that going to church
does not necessarily mean people are godly. They may have great intentions,
but the enemy comes in to kill steal and destroy—and he can and will use
some of the strongest Christians to do so.

That is not meant to discourage you in any way. It is to let you know
that the enemy is alive and well in this world. He will use anyone and
anything to tear down the Christian faith. However, we know who wins
in the end—and it's not Satan.

God is so good, and he is good all the time.

Some of us in the family experienced some very traumatic things, and
the only option we had was to forgive or leave. And if we stayed, we had
to try to let it go. We attempted to let it go, but you can't forget it once
it's in your mind.

A counselor once gave me the best advice. He said, "Go home, hash it
out, ask what you need to ask, get it out—all of it—and then never bring
it up again."

Is that possible? Yes. Is it hard? Yes! However, if you can't let it go and let it die, then it will kill you and everyone involved. *Codependency* is excessive emotional or psychological reliance on a partner, typically a partner who requires support due to an illness or addiction.

We tried to rebuild our lives, but I had so many struggles and insecurities. Codependency is so debilitating. The person's every thought and breath depends on whether the other person is happy or going back to his old ways. Did he love me anymore? I became so insecure that I would call him at work at least twenty times a day to see what he was doing, where he was, and who he was talking to.

After much counseling, prayer, and meetings, I have overcome that debilitating feeling. I did not want my kids to think that was how you were supposed to live. I was not setting the right example for them, and they would carry it into adulthood. Much of that codependency started at home due to the lack of stability in our home while they were growing up. The instability caused negative thoughts and insecurities. They saw the glass as half empty instead of half full. Codependency causes negative feelings all the time, and the person's trust in the Lord can grow or diminish.

When we were in the middle of our strongest trials, I told my husband I placed him on a pedestal and did everything I could do to be a good wife.

He informed me that he never asked to be put there.

That was quite an awakening for me because I had put him on a pedestal, but I worked very hard to make sure that never happened again. The mind can and will go to places that you can't imagine. You bargain; you imagine what someone has done, and then suddenly you realize you are   not crazy.

It took me a while to break my codependency, but I still struggle with it on occasion. Codependency is when you rely on someone else's emotions or actions to rule your mood or your demeanor. It affects every aspect of how you react and respond to the other person's mood. Half the time, it feels like you're crazy or out of control. However, you can overcome that by becoming an interdependent couple that depends equally on one another.

It will take a while because it's a process. It takes a lot of work, but you can overcome it. I spent a lot of time at my dad's during that time. My daddy always made me feel secure and loved. Maybe I was a daddy's girl. Starlet and I looked after him much of the time after Momma died. I always made Starlet think she was his favorite, but I really was the favorite, which is a running joke between us.

No matter how good or bad your upbringing was or how privileged you were, your parents are the only unconditional love you really have. Not every parent has it. We all know people who are not fit to be parents. They only know how to love themselves.

Daddy loved momma so much, and we truly thought we would lose him to grief. We watched him like a hawk, and he surprised us all. About eight years later, he began to drink more hard liquor and abuse Percodan. We were angry because he would drive that way or light a cigarette and then drop it. My sister put a piece of asbestos that goes under wood-burning stoves under his chair so the house would not catch on fire.

Daddy began to get sicker. We thought it was the pills and alcohol, but we knew more might be wrong when he started having other bad symptoms.

The doctor was sure it was an ulcer. After they opened him up, they closed him back up and informed us that he had cancer that had already spread. We felt bad about griping at him so much. We even had him admitted to rehab prior to the diagnosis, and that incident devastated him. I regret that terribly; he was using the alcohol and pills because of the cancer. He refused treatment since he was in his eighties.

The scariest part for me was that I didn't think my dad knew the Lord. I never pushed him because of his age. I just prayed he would come to know Christ before it was too late. One of my sisters and I traded out weekends with him to give each other a break. She bought the house from him so she could take over the bills and take the stress off of him.

We were watching westerns on one of my weekends, and he said, "Baby, do you think your preacher would come out and talk to me?"

Oh, my goodness! I am not sure I ever dialed the phone faster than I did at that moment.

When the preacher came over after church on Sunday, I went into the kitchen to give them privacy. My dad told the pastor that he had been a man who liked to drink too much, had made many mistakes, and was not a good man. He asked if Jesus could love and accept a man like him at his age.

The pastor took him down the road of salvation and explained that none of us were worthy except through the love of Christ.

My dad accepted Jesus in his heart right then and there.

I felt such joy in my heart. My prayers had been answered after all that time. The day would soon come that my daddy went to be with the Lord. When I looked at him for the last time, I knew I would see him again in heaven. Even after all these years, I still miss him. Many o people have lost their parents, it doesn't matter their age no one is ever ready to lose the people they love.

After about a year, I felt like I could not stand it anymore. I emotionally fell apart. As I was getting ready for work, I was so depressed. I went into my closet and found myself in constant prayer. I was begging the Lord for peace. I needed it so desperately.

All of a sudden, it felt like a cold pitcher of water had been poured on my head. It went from the top of my head to the tip of my toes. I walked out of the closet that day with a peace that passes all understanding. He had mercy on me and heard my cries.

He will wipe away every tear from their eyes, and death shall be no more, neither shall there be mourning, nor crying, nor pain anymore, for the former things have passed away."
—Angels Looking After PeopleGod Will Keep
SafeAngels Providing Protection
Heaven And AngelsCharge

Revelation 21:4 (NIV)

CHAPTER 19

Attack of the Body Snatchers

That was the beginning of a massive amount of health problems for me, and there would be even more hardship to endure. Many of the health issues ran in my family, and I am thankful that my kids and grandkids have been healthy so far. I pray they stay that way.

I am still reaching for God's hand and holding onto it, but I felt him slipping away many times. In reality, I was the one who was slipping away. While Daddy was still alive, I had major stomach issues. Since he had already been diagnosed with stomach cancer, we were afraid I had the same condition. Glory to God it wasn't, but I did end up with a major corrective surgery. When it eventually failed, my stomach issues returned. I have always worked and contributed to our family income; it might not have been much, but it was what it was.

When our oldest daughter was sixteen, she told us she was pregnant and wanted to get married. Our first granddaughter came along soon after they were married. She couldn't have been any cuter; she was a little toot who stole our hearts right away.

After not much longer, baby number two arrived. Nobody was expecting that little surprise, but our hearts melted again. They split up, which led our daughter into a life of chaos, drugs, and bad relationships.

She asked if the girls could come live with us. With no hesitation—and believing it was temporary—we took them with happy hearts.

However, I quit my job because day care was way too expensive. The youngest was not healthy and required a lot of medical attention. Our daughter was in a relationship that did not allow her to come around much. She was living in a really bad situation, and she became pregnant with our first grandson. She tried to remove herself from that life and that relationship, but it dragged on for about three more months.

She woke up one morning and realized the baby had not woken up to eat. When she reached to pull him to her, he was stiff and cold. He had succumbed to sudden infant death syndrome. An autopsy confirmed the cause of death. That finally released her to leave that relationship and begin to rebuild her life with her two girls.

After his death, she dug into everything there was to know about SIDS. She eventually went to nursing school and met her future husband, who has been one of her greatest blessings. They have been married for sixteen years, and they had a son together. She got her life on track, and her family is doing great. The death of that grandchild set much of her transformation in motion. Do you ever wonder if you're on a really crazy ride and whether it is ever going to stop spinning? That was where we all were at that point.

> Therefore a man shall leave his father and his mother and
> hold fast to his wife, and they shall become one flesh.
> —Genesis 2:24 (NIV)

CHAPTER 20

Meet the Family

Much to our surprise, our eighteen-year-old was about to marry her high school sweetheart. They were pregnant. I also had a reoccurrence of the cancer for the third time. I was so scared, and my daughter was pregnant. All I could do was pray. I said, "Lord, please let me live long enough to hold my grandbaby."

In June, I got an all clear on my cancer.

When my granddaughter was born in August, I called her my angel baby because God had heard my cries. She is now eighteen, and I still call her "Angel." That has always been my name for her. She knows what it means, and she even put her name in my phone as "Your Angel Baby."

Fourteen months later, we were blessed with yet another granddaughter. She is a little pistol. She is sixteen now, and she will give you the "what for" if you mess with anyone she loves. Fortunately, our grandkids have been raised in church. To the best of my knowledge, all have accepted Christ except the youngest who is too young to comprehend yet. They waited about two years and decided to have one more child. That little boy has a heart for the Lord—and what a servant he is. I look for him to do mighty things for Christ.

Then, out of nowhere, our daughter was hit with a divorce after ten years of marriage. She and the children were devastated, but they made it through. "But if the unbelieving partner separates, let it be so. In such cases the brother or sister is not enslaved. God has called you to peace" (1 Corinthians 7:15).

Our youngest daughter is active in anything she can get in. Her personality is just like her dad's, and they still butt heads. She worked with her dad for most of her teen years, and she could build a house. At nineteen, she decided she wanted to get married—but she didn't want kids. The Lord had something different in mind because six months after the wedding, she found out she was pregnant.

I thought, *Oh, my goodness. She doesn't want kids. What kind of mom will she be?*

All it took was that baby boy kicking in her belly. Thirteen months later, she had a daughter who is just like me in many ways. Two years later, she had another daughter, and two years after that, the caboose—a little boy—came along. With four babies, she loves every second of motherhood. However, after thirteen years of marriage, she would be facing a divorce.

I asked the Lord *why* so many times, but the answers never seem to come. All I could see was the pain and devastation in their eyes and their hearts. My heart ached for the grandkids every day, and they all finally seemed to have their lives on track. There are a few thorns here and there, but I am a very proud momma. Regardless of any mistakes or shortcomings they may have, they are mine. I am proud to be who the Lord picked to have them as my children and grandchildren. I am so thankful for all ten of them. I pray God's hand stays upon them at all times. "He said to them, 'Because of your hardness of heart, Moses allowed you to divorce your wives, but from the beginning it was not so'" (Matthew 19:8 NIV).

As the baby of six kids, I was sheltered in many ways by two of my sisters. But because I always relied on them to take care of things, I became known as the little sister who was weak. They thought I had been through so much that I was just too fragile to go through any more trauma. If they only knew the trauma I never told them about. I never believed I had the grit it would take to stand up for myself or fight for what I wanted—not even to fight for my life. I was programmed to believe I was too fragile, especially after my first husband passed away.

Just to set the record straight, I am not weak. I have endured more than most people have ever gone through in their lives. With God carrying me, I have endured childhood tragedy, the loss of my parents, a brother, a son, a grandson, and a husband—and I was about to go through more life-changing events. Am I weak? I think not!

CHAPTER 21

The Ministry

God is not unjust; he will not forget your work and the love you have
shown him as you have helped his people and continue to help them.
—Hebrews 6:10 (NIV)

Here is the reality of life in the ministry. Anyone who tells you the ministry
is working one day a week and drawing a paycheck obviously doesn't have
a clue about what it takes. You are counselor, a fixer, a maintenance man,
a builder, a doctor, and whatever else people need—even an entertainer.
It's definitely not a bed of roses, but it can be very rewarding—and you're
building the kingdom for the Lord.

We have been emotionally crushed by so-called friends and coworkers
in the church. We have been lied to and looked down on. Look at what Paul
and the other disciples endured! Most of all, look what Christ endured. We
are in no comparison with any of them, all you can do is try your best and
try to learn from your experiences. Phillipians 1:6-11 Being confident of
this very thing that He who has begun a good work in you will complete
it until the day of Jesus Christ.

Don't give up on God or the people he has called you to serve. Stay the
course. Life is too short and hell is too hot to allow discouragement to turn
into defeat! If he brought you to it, he will lead you through it.

I won't go into much about the ministry because I do not want to
make Christianity appear useless or hopeless. It is and should be the most
important thing in your life. People in life let you down in the church

and in the world. We just hold one another accountable as brothers and sisters in Christ.

It's an amazing journey that you don't want to miss out on. As Christians, do we profile others? On one Sunday evening service, as the pastor was in the middle of his lesson, a homeless man walked in. He wore jeans, boots, and a denim vest, and he had a long white beard and very few teeth. As he began to walk down the aisle, we could hear the clanging of metal. As he approached the front, he turned around—and all we could see was knives. Knives were everywhere. They were even dangling off chains attached to his belt loops.

The pastor never wavered.

I thought we were about to be robbed or killed, but all he wanted was to share the Word. He was newly sober, and he wanted to rededicate himself to God. He also wanted to sing a song for us.

We made it through unscathed, and our new friend became a permanent fixture in our church. He was always encouraging others. Don't judge a book by its cover—and you may get a Daniel in your life too.

There may be the occasion in your church life when you get hurt by someone or something, or there may be a disagreement over the color of the paint. Remember that those are temporal things; you are placed in your place of worship to serve. Being a member of a church is not about what the church can do for you; it should be what you can do for the kingdom. If you are doing anything for self-gratification or notice you're in it for the wrong reasons, remain in your area of service, do your best in it, and wait for the blessings to reign down on you.

There are always trials, but our goal is use the gift the Lord has blessed us with. We all have one or more gifts. We have served in the ministry with many strikes against us, but the Lord still uses us. We came through drug addiction, alcoholism, abuse, and divorce. We are broken vessels, but the Potter picks up our broken pieces and puts them back together. Yes, we have scars and cracks, but when the Potter fixes them, there are no leaks. We are just vessels that are ready to be filled again.

We have made long-lasting relationships with our Christian families. We have loved and lost many as well. However, we go through life with the idea that church people are not capable of hurting or doing others wrong.

They are human and make mistakes just like the rest of us do. Forgiveness is the key to our lives and being meaningful in the Lord's eyes.

Think about the galaxy the heavens, the stars, and the vastness of it all. Isn't it amazing what God's creation is made of? We are a part of that, what a privilege. Our lives are meaningless without the Lord. Christ has always has been the center of the universe, the Creator, the I AM, and that is good enough for me.

In the garden, the army fell back at the mention of the I Am. "When Jesus said, 'I am He, they drew back and fell to the ground" (John 18:6). If that's not power, I don't know what is!

As we continued in the ministry, my health began to decline. It started with stomach issues, but I always thought it was just stress. I had a surgery that would set a series of surgeries in motion. It began with testing to make sure I did not have what my dad had. When it was determined that I didn't, they decided to pursue a corrective surgery, which failed within six weeks. That was in 1995, which was also when we were having so many marital problems.

After I made it through that surgery, we went on with life. However, the relationship problems I thought were over began again. We began to work things out, but it was a hurtful, long process.

By 2004, I was having many more serious medical issues, and I went to a different doctor for a second opinion. He told me it was the only surgical option for me. They could try a revision or gastric bypass, which would reroute the acid in my body and lessen my chances of having esophageal cancer. The process would also result in necessary weight loss. A decision that would change my life and health from then to now.

Don't give up on God or the people he has called you to serve. Stay the course, you may feel at times your in this wonderful thing called life alone, but Never forget or believe that lie, you are never alone Christ promise to us is He will never leave us or forsake us.

Six months later, I needed to have incisional hernia repair with a mesh placement. The pain was worse than either of the other surgeries.

In January 2006, I had to have another hernia repair with a mesh placement. It was an epic fail, but I was determined to have no more surgeries. I had already been through my fair share, and I wanted no more. Alas, that was not to be. The worst was yet to come.

CHAPTER 22

Almost Dead

We were hard at work in the ministry. Cal and I did a little travel nursing, and we saw some areas of our great nation we had never seen. When we got back, we settled back into regular life again.

The Lord called on us to begin a church from scratch, and we eventually grew out of two buildings. We decided to move to a different location and do some remodeling. We leased an old gymnasium behind an existing church and merged the two churches where there were only about six members left. We continued to grow, and God blessed that ministry. It was primarily for those with a past and those who were hurting or down and out. We attracted those people because Cal would share his testimony, and they would see that there might still be hope for them.

We were there through many difficulties, and we served the Lord there for fourteen years. When we left, Cal decided to retire due to my declining health. I had been diagnosed with atrial fibrillation, which is an irregularity in the heartbeat. I was put on medication and was good for a while. I had a few flare-ups here and there but nothing major. When I began to have trouble with my stomach again, the doctors wanted nothing to do with me because they were stumped.

In 2014, I began a journey like none other in my life. I went into the hospital with an atrial fibrillation episode, and they had to chemically start and stop my heart. They wanted to keep me for observation because I had been unable to keep food down for a while. The hospitalist came in and seriously expressed to me that I needed to expand outside of our scope of doctors and try a larger hospital with doctors who specialized in high-risk patients.

I really didn't know what to say. I had been there for my heart, and after more tests, she came back with the news. I was self-diagnosing cancer or something incurable. I knew she was afraid to tell me I was dying.

She gave me the name of a good high-risk surgeon in Dallas

A surgeon?

I was reeling from the news and was not sure what to do. I had an appointment with Dr. J in two weeks; seeing him that quickly was unheard of. We were not sure what to expect. We were praying for a Christian doctor, and all we could do was wait.

When I met the doctor, I was as nervous as a cat on a hot tin roof. When the tall Indian doctor in his early fifties walked in, I could tell he had thoroughly reviewed my health history. There were red marks all over the pages. He visited with us long enough to tell me he was going to fix my problem. I would go through some tests, and he would do the surgery in two weeks.

I felt like I had a hurricane in my head. I said, "So, Dr. J, just how risky is this surgery?"

He informed me that it would be very risky due to the amount of surgeries I had already had. He added, "I am just God's vessel, and I can only do what God has planned for you."

I grabbed his arm gently and asked, "Are you a Christian?"

He smiled and said, "Yes, Mrs.Smith, I serve the risen Savior, Jesus Christ!"

We left there with so much peace. It meant so much to know God was in control. For two weeks, we drove back and forth to Dallas for all the tests.

On morning of the surgery, Dr. J came in to talk to me right before they put me out. He said a prayer with me, held my hand, and made the symbol of the cross on my hand and forehead.

"Bless the LORD, O my soul, and forget not all his benefits, who forgives all your iniquity, who heals all your diseases" (Psalm 103:2, 3).

The surgery ended up being far more complicated than we could have ever imagined. I woke up praising the Lord for allowing me to wake up such a high-risk surgery.

Dr. J came in later to tell me what he had done. As he was ready to close up, the Lord impressed on him to look in a different area. He found the balled-up mesh from 2006 and 2007, which had migrated and was pressing on my diaphragm. I would have been dead in six months to a year!

Within twelve hours, things changed drastically. I needed the Lord to intervene for me more than ever.

CHAPTER 23

What Happened to the Time?

When we feel anxious and afraid we can take comfort in
knowing that God is reaching out His hand to us to help
us trust Him and walk with Him. While anxiety can feel
overpowering or terrifying, we should not fear, but rather trust
in the perfect and never-changing love and peace of God
—Isaiah 41:13

After twelve hours of feeling decent, considering I had tubes everywhere, I
began to go into respiratory failure. I was delirious and was asking if people
made it through whatever they were talking about. As they took me into
surgery, I thought Cal was cradling me and telling me I would be fine. I
was standing behind that scene, and I did not have a chance to think of it
again until I went home.

On our way home, I asked Cal if they let him go in when they inserted
the chest tube.

He looked at me and said, "Of course not."

I said, "Not even in the holding room?"

He assured me that he had not gone past the doors.

That was my Jesus moment! I knew without a doubt that Christ was
cradling me and comforting me.

They took me to surgery, placed a chest tube in my left lung, and brought me to the ICU.

The only thing I remember was the transfer from one bed to another. I was in and out, but my family filled me in later.

> Do not fear, for I am with you do not be dismayed, for I am your God. I will strengthen you and help you; I will uphold you with my righteous right hand. (Isaiah 41:10 NIV)

My lung collapsed, and they tried to reinflate it. When an infection set in, they could not even make an opening. It was as thick as glue, but they cultured it. Once they started the antibiotics, the lung started doing better. I ended up with five chest tubes because of the lung issues. I began to run a fever of 107 degrees. They packed me in ice for a few days while they tried to find the source of the problem.

I developed a leak at the surgical site, sending my body into sepsis. Severe sepsis infection can lead to the failure of the kidneys, lungs, and liver. It can also lead to death. A person with a severe sepsis infection can have symptoms including skin patches, weakness, unconsciousness, breathing problems, decreased urination, and low mental ability. I was in really bad shape, and they placed me on a breathing machine. They had to go in three times to repair it because I am a complicated patient. I was going against the grain of all the treatment.

I was in a medically induced coma, and I was in and out of consciousness. My husband never left my side since they let him stay in the ICU with me around the clock. He bathed me, exercised me, and did all of the things for me that would get me ready for when I came out of the coma. I only remember bits and pieces. Delirium can be caused by a combination of numerous factors, including surgery, infection, isolation, dehydration, poor nutrition, and medications such as painkillers, sedatives, and sleeping pills. I have few memories of waking up for brief periods of time, but then I went into a deeper coma. They called the family in three times and told them I would not make it.

But Dr. J and Cal would come together and pray over my body for healing every day. I was in a coma for thirty days and remained in the hospital even longer after that. I developed a ICU psychosis, which is a disorder when patients in an intensive care unit or a similar setting experience a cluster of serious psychiatric symptoms. ICU psychosis is also called ICU syndrome. ICU psychosis is a form of delirium or acute brain failure.

I clearly remember things that were so very true to me that never happened. It was a terrible experience that led to post-traumatic stress disorder. They would call my husband in from his room in the hospital, and he would run into the room, take my face in his hands, and say "It's okay, sweet pea."

They said I would automatically calm down.

I always felt paranoid when he left. I thought they were being mean and making him leave. My family grew a love and respect for him that they never had before. They saw the love he had for me, and they didn't have to worry about whether I was being taken care of.

PTSD develops in people who have experienced a shocking, scary, or dangerous event. The loss of time still bothers me. That's time I can't get back. I remember people coming to see me when I started waking up. I thought I was talking to people—my brain said I was—but I could not talk.

I tried to write something down once. A friend was scrambling to find something to write on, and when I went to write, there were only straight lines and crooked lines. I was just coherent enough to think, *What in the world, girl? You know how to write.*

It was time to start getting me out of the bed and into a chair.

I was excited to get up until she came in and said, "Okay. We going to stand up and turn around."

I thought it was going to be so easy, but it was quite the opposite. It would be a while before we began rehab, but it went well. I recovered, but I was very weak for such a long time.

It is natural to feel afraid during and after a traumatic situation. Fear triggers many split-second changes in the body to help defend against danger or avoid it. This fight-or-flight response is a typical reaction meant to protect a person from harm. Nearly everyone will experience a range of reactions after trauma, yet most people recover from initial symptoms naturally. Those who continue to experience problems may be diagnosed with PTSD. People who have PTSD may feel stressed or frightened even when they are not in danger.

> See now that I myself am He! There is no God besides Me. I put to death and I bring to life, I have wounded and I will heal, and no one can deliver out of My hand. (Deuteronomy 32:39)

The things your body can go through and how it begins to heal itself is nothing shy of a miracle. The Lord intricately allows the body to do its own amazing healing, He just uses doctors to help with the process.

When I left hospital that June, after two months I thought I was in a dream. Dr. J came into my room for discharge, looked at me, and held up two fingers. He said that after what my body had been through, I could expect at least a two-year recovery. What in the world happened to six weeks? You have surgery, you leave, and you're good to go in six weeks? Not me.

Two weeks later, I started coughing and not breathing well. We went back to the hospital and found out I had blood clots in my lungs and a secondary infection of whooping cough. I was kept in isolation, and I was released in about two weeks. It was June, and we were glad to be home. I went home with all sorts of tubes and a feeding tube.

Taking out the feeding tube was very painful because I had developed fistulas, which start inside the surgical cavity and tunnel to other areas. I was readmitted for observation in August, and they were watching me closely. When you're in the hospital for that long, you build a rapport with the staff. They were awesome. That visit was about a week, which began the pattern for the next three and a half years.

We had booked a trip to Alaska with some friends, but we put it off until the end of fishing season. I pushed for us to go so I could just get away. While we were there, I began to have odd symptoms. I ended up having to make a trip to the emergency room. I had a touch of pneumonia, but that was all they found. That was just a few days before we were heading home.

I started having some unusual pain in the center of my stomach, and it was beginning to protrude. In September 2014, we went back to Dallas to see what was going on. I had developed another infection in the stomach that required another mild surgical procedure.

After several days in the hospital, I asked Dr. J why it all seemed to be raining down on me.

He just prayed for me and showed so much compassion. I guess I was one of the lucky ones!

At that point, I began to question the Lord about why I was going through this over and over again. I was still very weak and was not myself mentally, and there was much more to come. I ended up with thirty-one hospital visits in three and a half years; all but four were for life-threatening conditions.

For a year after the initial surgery, I continued to have blood clots in my lungs. My doctor ended up referring me to a hematologist, and I was diagnosed with a rare clotting disorder that they don't even have a name for. I have a hyper coagulation disorder, and I have blood clots on every blood thinner except a daily injection that still puts me at risk. This is a thorn in the flesh that I have truly begged The Lord to remove, however like Paul apparently the answer is a no. So I go on every day with the knowledge of what may or may not happen due to this disorder. The key is not to let it rule my thoughts and my life.

I, like many others, live at risk daily on these lifesaving medications. I hate those injections, but I know I am blessed. At least they have something that can treat it.

I went into a deep depression. I was on so many medications, and I don't remember what half of them were for. They really never worked because I came out of the hospital as a chemically induced drug addict. I literally had to detox from the medication they had me on. When they sent me home with pain medication, it was like eating candy compared to what they gave me in the hospital. If one didn't work, maybe two or three would. With my family's addictive personalities, I realized this was going to become a problem if I didn't do something to stop it. "A man's spirit will endure sickness, but a crushed spirit who can bear?" (Proverbs 18:14).

I self-admitted myself into a behavioral health hospital/clinic to stop that process before it took over me. I was only getting about two or three hours of sleep per night, which certainly was not helping. Insomnia puts your body in many different states. I was embarrassed that I had to go into a physiatrist hospital, but it was the beginning of another healing process. I was able to be a witness there, but that was not why I went. I went for me, myself, and I—or so I thought. I had nobody else in mind, but the Lord did. While I was there I was able to bless others with a talent for painting The Lord has given me, and while doing so, I was able to witness to others as well. Sometime I wonder, if The Lord put me there for my healing or to help others.

CHAPTER 24

Healing Is a Slow Process

Why, my soul, are you downcast? Why so disturbed within me? Put
your hope in God, for I will yet praise him, my Savior and my God.
—Psalm 42:11

When it got closer to the end, I began to isolate myself. I didn't want to
go to the store. I didn't want to go to church or be out in public. I closed
myself off to everyone, and I didn't realize for a while that I was doing
that. That was a very scary place to be because I began to be a burden. I
thought nobody understood, but when I was around anyone, that was all
I could talk about.

I started coloring, and I had found tribal art coloring books in Alaska.
I thought it would help with my hand-eye coordination or take my mind
off the things I was going through. I began to color, and I got better and
better. The hospital allowed me to bring my colors to the hospital with me.

I was in the process of rehabbing myself and didn't realize it. I began to
minister to the people in there; by the time I left, everyone picked a picture
and had me personalize it to take with them. As they watched me color,
we would talk about our issues. That gave me an opportunity to witness
to those who were struggling with their faith or who had no faith. It was
time to go home. I believed I was better and was ready and able to cope
with life again, but that didn't quite work out. When I got home, I slowly
began to crawl back in my shell, I just could not get myself out of that rut.

My prayer life began to diminish, my relationships with my family were struggling and I just became a big mess.

The Lord is so merciful to me, and those pity parties I seemed to swim around in became more and more. I just could not get what had happened in my head, and asking The Lord WHY? I had been faithful, true, and loved Him for so very long, and then it hit me, Bad things happen to us all. As you go through this journey of life we have to remember that even though we are special to The Lord and we are His children that does not mean we won't suffer. One thing I was told early on was that many times when our brain goes through a trauma of that magnitude that it begins to help the rest of the body to begin to heal the problem is, when it does begin to reconnect it may not always go back together the way it was, and guess what mine didn't. So, I am trying to learn to live life with a new way of thinking and doing, and that is hard dear friends. But, My Father is with me and I have no doubt that the work He has begun in me will come to completion, in His time.

CHAPTER 25

I Am Not Normal

Here is a call for the endurance of the saints, those who keep
the commandments of God and their faith in Jesus.
—Revelation 14:12 (NIV)

I thought I was getting back to normal—at least what my normal was. I did well for a while, but as I was making the bed, I fell and snapped my Achilles tendon.

Dr. J had already told me it would be too dangerous to put me to sleep for surgery for at least two years, and it had only been a year. We had to argue with the doctor who wanted to put me under. He didn't want to do a block, but we convinced him to do a local anesthesia anyway.

My orthopedic surgeon said he never had anyone talk so much during a surgery. They had a hard time keeping me sedated. We got through that, but I ended up back in the hospital multiple times for various weird things that would just pop up. I began to think it was never going to end. Three months was the maximum length of time that I had not been admitted for one reason or another.

I continued in and out of the emergency rooms and the hospital. It was a constant thing for me, and I was tired of being sick!

In April 2017, I was going to take my first solo trip in three years to visit my sister. She lived seven hours away, and I made it to her house. She had been going through some health issues, and I wanted to be there for her. It was an amazing surprise and reunion. Our first day was awesome, and I got to be her helper instead of her waiting on me. We were enjoying our time, and I was enjoying a little freedom being away from home for a while and feeling some independence until my heart went into atrial fibrillation. I said nothing because I kept thinking it would calm down. I had been through all the prior issues without my heart messing up once. I finally told my sister on Thursday, and she told me to call the doctor.

> But they who wait for the LORD shall renew their strength;
> they shall mount up with wings like eagles; they shall run
> and not be weary; they shall walk and not faint. (Isaiah
> 40:31 NIV)

The doctor told me go straight to the hospital. Due to my blood disorder, I would be at a higher risk. My brother-in-law took me to the hospital, leaving my sick sister at home alone. The staff began an aggressive treatment to get my heart to convert, but after eighteen hours, it had not converted. The next day they airlifted me to a larger hospital. In the helicopter, I converted to a regular heartbeat. Cal came to get me, ending my short-lived freedom.

In July 2017, my heart decided to go back into A-fib. It took quite a while before it converted back. In August, I begin to develop bowel obstructions caused by scar tissues strangling the bowels. I had three in the month of August, but they kept reversing, which was a good thing.

On September 30, 2017, I was rushed to the hospital with a life threatening obstruction. A very arrogant doctor informed me that he had reviewed my file for about thirty minutes and would not touch me with a ten-foot pole. He thought cutting into me would be like cutting into concrete.

I couldn't comprehend why he was saying that. Even though I knew I was sick, we were not expecting that statement. I tried to stroke his ego and told him I didn't understand because I had heard he was one of the best surgeons in town.

He informed me that he *was* the best doctor by far, and since he was the best, he knew what he was talking about. If he did elect to do surgery on me, which he wouldn't, I would have a catastrophic event—such as a stroke or a heart attack—and most likely die. I *was* dying, and I needed to go home, get hospice in place, and begin to make the transition because no one would touch me.

We were devastated. We were not prepared for that news in any way, form, or fashion. Two friends heard him say that and act the way he acted, and they were appalled.

My husband insisted on waiting on our original surgeon, but when he came in, he said he concurred with the other doctor. Since the bowel appeared to be trying to unkink itself, they would let me go home in the morning.

As he walked out, my husband asked if I felt like it was easing off any or did I feel any better?

I told him there was no way, and he walked out of the room straight to the nurse's station and asked to speak with the hospitalist. The hospitalist came to the nurse's station, looked at my husband, and asked what he needed him to do.

My husband gave him Dr. J's number since he knew the ins and outs of my insides. When they reached him, he told them to get me in an ambulance and get me to Dallas immediately. The arrangements were made, and I was gone in no time.

The doctors at home had told us I was dying—and there was no hope!

The Lord will keep you from all harm—he will watch over your life; the Lord will watch over your coming and going both now and forevermore.
—Psalm 121:7–8 (NIV)

CHAPTER 26

There Is Hope

You restored me to health and let me live. Surely it was
for my benefit that I suffered such anguish. In Your
love You kept me from the pit of destruction; Y
ou have put all my sins behind your back.
—Isaiah 38:17 (NIV)

I wish I could say the ambulance ride was pleasant, but all I remember is
how sick I was. They were trying to keep me as comfortable as possible,
but I was getting worse by the minute. The Dallas traffic was a trip, but
they were doing all they could for me.

At the hospital in Dallas, we bypassed everyone. They knew I was
coming and were waiting. It was late in the evening, and my middle sister,
brother-in-law, oldest daughter, and son-in-law got there just in time. They
didn't know if they were saying goodbye or what. Our youngest was caught
in traffic and got there just as they took me back.

Dr. J and his team started prepping me for surgery immediately.

I told him that the doctors at home told me I was not going to make it.

His response blew me away. He informed me that he was not the best
doctor, which I didn't believe, but he did work for the ultimate physician,
Jesus Christ, and we would see what He thought about that!

As I woke up in ICU, I was not quite sure of my surroundings. I
opened my eyes and realized I had made it out of surgery. The Lord said,
"You always have hope."

Since our God is the God of hope we who represent Him to this hopeless world must be people of hope—not mere optimists, but people filled with hope because of the certainty of God's promises in Christ.

It would take three visits in the next three months to totally comprehend what that word would come to mean to me! Hope is a powerful word! Approximately a month later, I landed back in the hospital with a secondary infection from the surgery in September. I thought that was the case when I was in the hospital for a week on antibiotics, but they sent me home on wound care. I continued to get worse, and the wound got larger.

The wound-care specialist took one look and said, "Oh, no. This will require surgery."

I went back to my hospital in northeast Texas for another surgery. Each time I had surgery, my chances of survival dropped. I pulled through only by the grace of God.

After another week in the hospital, I went home with wound care again. That time, my wound-care nurse was amazing and watched me like a hawk. The two-to-three-month recovery lasted six weeks, which was a shock to me since I always had such a hard time healing. All the honor and glory for healing goes to my Father in heaven. Obviously, the Lord has something for me to do because he has brought me through so very much and had shown me such favor, which I do not deserve.

Isaiah 41:10 tells us that we don't need to be afraid: "Do not fear, for I am with you; do not be dismayed, for I am your God. I will strengthen you and help you; I will uphold you with my righteous right hand."

My fear was not how I thought I would handle things. I really thought my faith was stronger. I knew the Lord only wanted good for me, but the fear rushed in like a mighty roaring wind. I still find myself falling into that fear when I feel a pain, when I can't breathe well, or when my vitals are off. The rebuilding of my faith continues to be a daily walk of faith and hope in Christ.

In September, I believe I had my miracle. I woke up with a message from the Lord: "Don't give up on your hope."

I knew I had to share what the Lord had done in my life. That particular surgery would lead to hospital stays in October 2017 and November 2017. During my last stay in the hospital, one of the chaplains stopped by my room, graciously introduced himself, and told me that my name was not on his list. Nevertheless, he went to my room and asked my name. I told him my name, and he looked at me and said, "Well, I need to tell you first of all this has never happened to me before, but the Lord stopped me in front of your door, and I was impressed upon to deliver a message to you."

I looked at him and said, "I would love to hear his message."

"The Lord said not to give up on your hope."

I began to cry, and he said, "I am guessing this has meaning to you."

I told him it did.

He asked if I would tell him what it meant to me.

I told him about what had happened in September, and he looked at me and said, "I get the feeling there is more to your story."

I smiled and said. "Well, you might be able to say that."

He asked for an explanation.

I tried to cut it short because there is so much to tell.

He told me I must have a strong background of faith and belief in the Lord to have gone through all the things I have endured.

I briefly shared that my life did not start out that way at all, and another brief explanation followed.

He looked at me with tears in his eyes and said, "Has anyone ever told you should write a book?"

I laughingly said, "Yes. I have had people tell me that, but I never took it seriously."

He thought that that could be the reason he was so impressed to stop by my room that day.

With pen and paper in hand, I began to write. My abilities have been extremely limited in my thinking, typing, and writing processes, but the Lord has set my hands on fire and given me the words to say. The process had begun and I had a deadline to meet. The writing of this book however small it may seem, took a lot of soul searching and a healing of sorts. As I found the publishing company I would choose and began a final edit, once again I landed in the hospital in February 2018. I had stayed up a whole night with leg pain and it had me a bit worried so being that I had been to the hospital so much I was just going to get checked to make sure it wasn't a blood clot. Well, naturally it was but that wasn't the big concern it seemed. The doctor came in to explain that the

IVC filter that was in me to prevent big clots from passing had broken and punctured my Aorta. Which is your main blood vein. It seems as The Lord would have so intricately make our bodies the Aorta has three layers a tough outer layer then a second safety layer, then the main which if punctured you would bleed out in minutes. The "strut" or leg of the filter had pierced the first layer and about to go through the second layer. We are transferring you straight to the hospital to surgery it must come out. Needless to say, here we go again. All of that being said obviously The Lord showed me great favor once again they attempted retrieval on that filter three times all total the third was the charm, as the doctor light heartedly told me you were sporting a Volkswagen now your sporting a Cadillac. Although a very traumatic experience my doctors for that procedure especially Dr. I was amazing. The Lord has seen me through many tragedies, many hurts, habits and hang-ups. Am I the same person, absolutely not! I can only pray that I can live for The Lord and bring Him honor and glory in all I say and do to even earn a drop of what He has given me and that is MY LIFE, Yes, I could say so much more about my life in general, but I have written what the Lord instructed me to write—for this go-around. This is not a feel-sorry-for-me book. This is not a pity party book or a health-comparison book. It's a book of hope! It's to encourage you that no matter what your life deals you—verbal or physical abuse, abandonment issues, alcoholism, drug addiction, death of a loved one, or health issues—you can overcome because God has overcome the world.

Is it easy? No, but it is possible. But you can't do any of this without Christ. It's hard enough to go through life feeling like you're alone with no one to turn to. Fortunately, I had a loving family that stuck right beside me. Whether you have family, friends, or someone else, you still have someone to turn to. His name is Jesus, and he loves you and wants you to fight and live a life that is full. Yes, you may be riddled with illness or hardship, but what is that truly in the light of eternity? You can feel sorry for yourself like I did, and you can contemplate ending your agony like I did. There are many things that cross our minds that we know are not of the Father, but we listen to them anyway. Do us both a favor and say this with me: "I choose to break this vicious cycle of being the victim, but I choose to conquer those obstacles in my life and become the victor because I am worth the effort." And always know you have a story within you too!

> For everyone who has been born of God overcomes the world.
> And this is the victory that has overcome the world—our faith.
> —1 John 5:4 (NIV)

Printed in the United States
By Bookmasters